ISBN 978-0-9887133-1-4

THE CHRISTMAS BUTTERFLY
a true story

WRITTEN BY F. MICHAEL SMITH
ILLUSTRATED BY CAROLYN LOMBARDO

DESIGNED BY DAWN CONROY

Dedicated to
Those who are gone,
Those yet to come,
...and to those who carry on.

It's hard into January and the white winter wonderland that was December is now just a cold, brittle gray. The hustling holiday haze has been replaced by a calm resignation to the dark and uncertain months ahead, before spring awakens the senses once again.

I sit on the living room sofa across from the new plastic smelling widescreen which, on this rare occasion, sits dark. I sit there staring at a seven foot Concolor pine which, several weeks ago, was our beautifully adorned Christmas tree- the centerpiece of our holiday season. It now stands barren except for a decorative silken strand of butterflies, tattered from time.

Unlike many who can't wait to dispose of the Tannenbaum pine, or remand the plastic version to the attic, we keep our tree watered and enjoy it until past the Epiphany, perhaps feeling sorry for the three Magi who seem to miss out on all the fun. Being nothing religious except maybe religiously tardy, it seems to us a good excuse to let the season linger just a bit longer.

C. Lombardo
2005

The holiday season offers us the time to reflect. Last year had not been the best of years with nagging ills, world concerns and the haunting of dreams gone by.

My wife, Marilee, whose name conveys her nature, has always kept our home a sanctuary of warmth and smiles. Although her parents are gone, their love and memories can be found throughout our house especially at Christmas. Her mother was not just a teacher but an educator in its highest form. She mentored her students through transformation into transcendence, from a cocoon born caterpillar into a butterfly, a creature of beauty and purpose.

Indeed, she had a special place in her heart for butterflies and suggested we think of her whenever butterflies graced our presence.

So fittingly, amongst the lights and decorations, our Christmas tree is always adorned with the aforementioned strand of silk butterflies. This garland is usually the last to depart our tree and brings me back to the title of this story.

I sit here waiting. It was a year ago at this time when it happened. It had been just another holiday season filled with anticipation along with the usual excesses of niceties and eggnog.

Chicago was as pretty as can be, all dressed up in her holiday finest topped with snow hoping the lighted trim and wrapping would hide the plain and empty. Yes, it was just another holiday... another meaningless celebration.

Our tree was still in its stand, naked of ornamental decorations. Remarkably, it had kept its needles and had actually sprouted fresh green buds. We were so stricken by this remarkable rebirth that we had delayed the inevitable.

So it was, as I sat there that morning, my attention was drawn sharply to a dark object moving beneath the tree. Startled, my fear turned to curiosity as my squinting eyes revealed it to be an oddly shaped insect ambling towards me.

After a few steps, it hesitated, then, a second or two later, its body unfolded, revealing wings which slowly opened and closed. Was it a moth? Another opening of its wings produced such beauty that I realized, to my amazement, it was a butterfly!

Lombardo

Our house came alive with this arrival, and I quickly devised a makeshift home for our guest. Days followed as we marveled at such a winged gift in the depths of winter.

Our early attempts at feeding were met with a total lack of interest. Rotten bananas and oranges were met with indifference.

Finally our growing concern was relieved with a helpful relative's concoction of sugar water on a sponge which proved successful.

Research revealed our winged friend to be a Black or Indra Swallowtail whose life normally consists of 10 glorious days of flight and love.

We resigned ourselves to a short visit but enjoyed each day, hoping our visitor found some level of enjoyment as it sipped sugar and spread its wings.

After two weeks, our wonder became tinged with sadness, as we prepared ourselves for the inevitable departure.

It was then that we heard about the Peggy Notebaert Nature Museum and Butterfly Habitat in Chicago's Lincoln Park area.

We packed up our little miracle to deliver him into freedom at this sun-filled haven to thousands of butterflies of all colors and shapes.

Upon entering, we were besieged by curious children wondering if we had a pet butterfly. My wife responded that such a magical creature could not be a pet but had graced our home for a brief visit. When asked how this could possibly be, she simply said, "It's a Christmas Butterfly."

C. Lombardo

As we entered the butterfly garden, I carefully placed our delicate visitor onto my arm and waited for flight. Seconds passed before he took off. Hovering briefly around my wife, he fluttered off disappearing into a sea of color and wings.

To this day, I don't know why tears blurred my vision and did not stop until the chill of winter air chastened my mood.

We drove home in silence, each reflecting on this extraordinary day.

So here I sit...waiting...contemplating. I sweep up countless needles and concede that it's time for this year's tree to find its final resting place deep in the backyard. I sigh with acceptance that a reoccurrence may never come to be.

I reminisce about that day in the butterfly habitat and the wonder and excitement that our visitor had caused the children to experience. I ponder how its silent presence had so touched my wife and me. I question if it was the butterfly or a universal hope and belief in the extraordinary that this winged traveler had triggered.

Some may have met this event with indifference. But not all of us. Some may choose, as I do, to believe it had a deeper meaning. Whether it was this creature or the inspiration it evoked doesn't matter.

C. Lombardo

C.Lombardo

Whether it was a sorely needed visit from a beloved spirit or a simple random sign of nature's wonder does not matter.

What matters is the occurrence... the gift of allowing my faith to breathe, if only for a moment, believing that something so simple could permit us to know and love the wonder of it.

And it struck me that we all need to be touched, if just for a moment, by gifts such as this.

Somewhere across this country, somewhere in the dead of winter, there will be a cocoon in a pine tree, and inside a sleeping wonder waiting to be born. And by some miracle or mistake of nature, a small beautiful creature who thrives on the warm renewal of spring may be born too early. But it might arrive just in time to fill a heart with joy, to rekindle a state of mind we left so long ago, and to remind us of how simple and wondrous God can be...

one butterfly at a time.

ABOUT THE AUTHOR

F. Michael Smith has been involved in the music business for many years. This singer-songwriter spends each Christmas with his wife in a 19th century English cottage just outside of Chicago. You can contact him at fmsmith.net.

A portion of the proceeds from sales of this book will go to the Salvation Army.

ABOUT THE ILLUSTRATOR

Carolyn Lombardo became an award-winning artist in the Chicago area after developing her talents from a desire to capture the essence of her own children. With a B.S. and M.A. in Education, she utilizes her creativity to this day, teaching children with special needs.

The art in this book has been inspired by and is dedicated to her nephew, Jared.

www.ingramcontent.com/pod-product-compliance
Lightning Source LLC
Chambersburg PA
CBHW041959100426
42813CB00019B/2929